STARTERS
LONG AGO
BOOKS

The Pyramid
Builders

Macdonald Educational

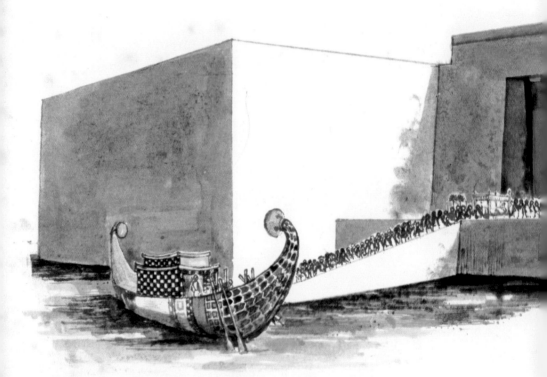

Here is the entrance to a pyramid
beside the River Nile.
The Nile is in Egypt.
Long ago the Egyptians built many pyramids
along the Nile.

pyramid

When an Egyptian king died,
he was put inside a pyramid.
His treasure was put in with him.
His body was brought to the pyramid
in a big ship.

mummy

Egyptians wanted dead bodies to last.
First they packed the body in salt.
Later they soaked it in oils.
Then they bandaged it.
The bandaged body was called a mummy.

4

mummy   mummy case   coffin

The mummy was put in a mummy case.
The mummy case fitted into a big coffin.
The coffins were put into the pyramid.

ramp

Pyramids were built like this.
Workers pulled stones up a ramp of earth.
The ramp climbed round the pyramid.
As the pyramid grew,
the ramp was made higher.

6

mason

Masons worked at the pyramid.
They measured the slabs of stone.
Then they cut the stones to fit together.

obelisk

Egyptians also put up pillars called obelisks.
Obelisks were carved and painted with writing.
The writing on them told a story in pictures.

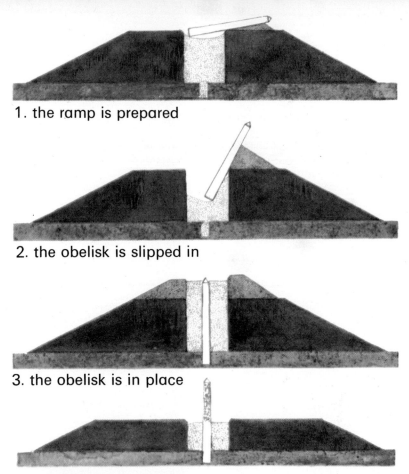

1. the ramp is prepared

2. the obelisk is slipped in

3. the obelisk is in place

4. the obelisk is carved and
   the ramp is removed

This is how an obelisk was put up.
They used a ramp to get it into place.
Then the obelisk was carved and painted.

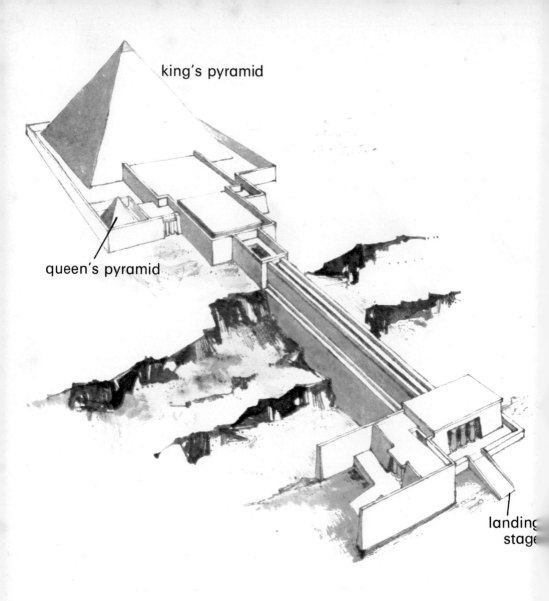

king's pyramid

queen's pyramid

landing
stage

Sometimes pyramids were built for families.
The biggest pyramid was for the king.
His family were in smaller pyramids around it.

10

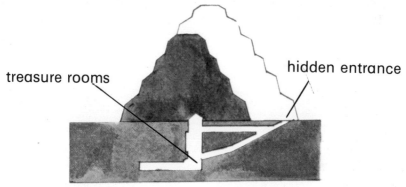

treasure rooms

hidden entrance

"step" pyramid of Zoser

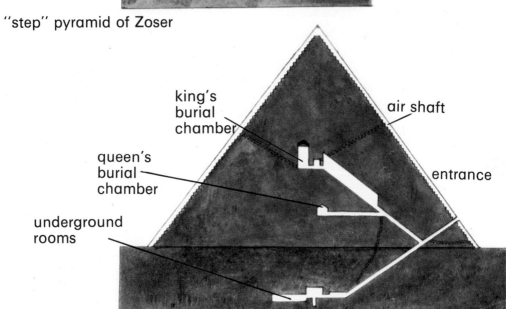

king's burial chamber

air shaft

queen's burial chamber

entrance

underground rooms

pyramid of Cheops

Big pyramids had many rooms inside.
Here are pictures showing the inside of
two pyramids.
One shows all the rooms.
The other shows a hidden entrance.

the entrance to
Tutankhamun's tomb

Long ago most of the treasures were stolen
from the pyramids.
But nobody stole from Tutankhamun's tomb.

12

chair

bed

stool

drinking cup

slippers

necklace

earrings

Here are some of Tutankhamun's treasures.
They were found a few years ago.
They tell us about life in Ancient Egypt.

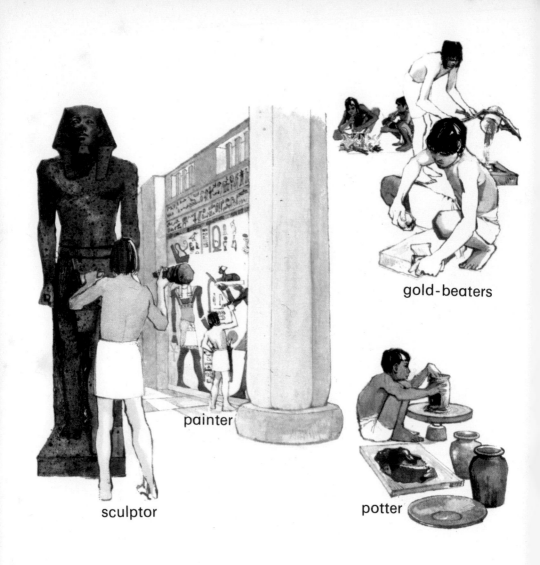

gold-beaters

painter

sculptor

potter

These men made some of the treasures.
The painter decorated the walls of the tomb.
Egyptians usually painted people facing sideways.

14

Bast

Osiris   Horus

Amun

Hathor

Anubis

Egyptians made statues of their gods.
Many Egyptian gods had animal heads.

papyrus
reeds

palette

scrolls

Most people in Egypt could not write.
They asked scribes to write for them.
Scribes wrote on paper
made from papyrus plants.
Papyrus plants grew beside the Nile.

16

palette

papyrus

scroll

to write

mountains

to build

water

rain

meadow

a million

to dance

Here are some Egyptian words and numbers.
They are really little pictures.
Some of the pictures are in groups.
Together they make a word.

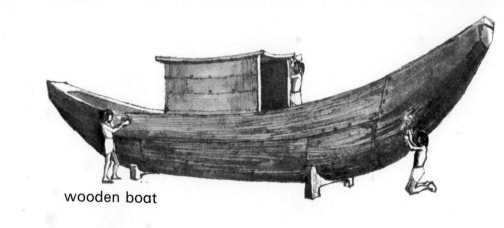

wooden boat

papyrus boat

Model boats have been found in tombs.
Egyptians had several kinds of boat.
Some were made of papyrus plants.
Others were made from wood.

18

One queen of Egypt
sent ships to explore the world.
This ship sailed along the coast of Africa.
It brought back treasures for the queen.

wig

Egyptian queens had many precious jewels.
This queen wore a wig.
She wore make-up too.

20

arrow quiver

spear
quiver

reins

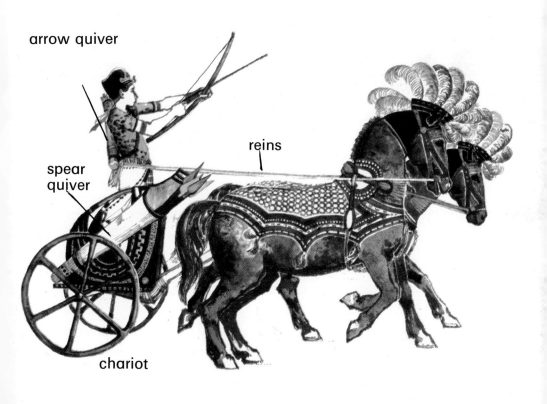

chariot

Egyptian soldiers wore simple armour.
The captains rode into battle in chariots.
This captain tied the reins to his belt.
Then he could use both hands to fight.

Sometimes Egyptians hunted birds.
This man is hunting with his cat.
The cat will fetch the bird
when his master has hit it.

shadoof

water well

Egypt is a very hot, dry country.
Farmers used shadoofs to water their land.
They dipped the shadoof into the river or the well.
They poured the water from it on to the fields.

23

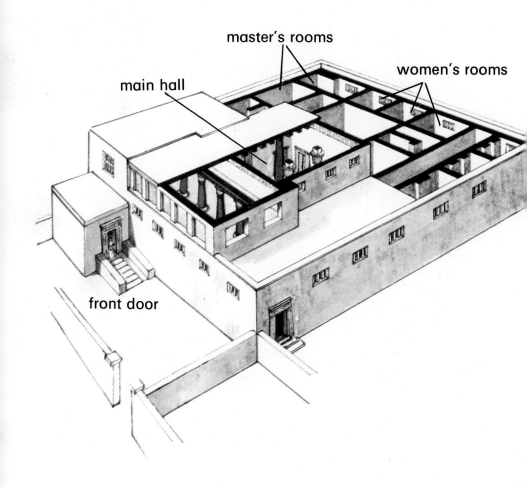

master's rooms

women's rooms

main hall

front door

This was the house of a rich Egyptian.
The house had many rooms.
It had a courtyard in the middle.
The kitchens were at the back.

24

Poor people lived in houses made of mud.
They spent most of the day outside.
The women even did the cooking outside.

clay

paints

See if you can make an obelisk.
Model it in clay.
You could make one out of wood.

26

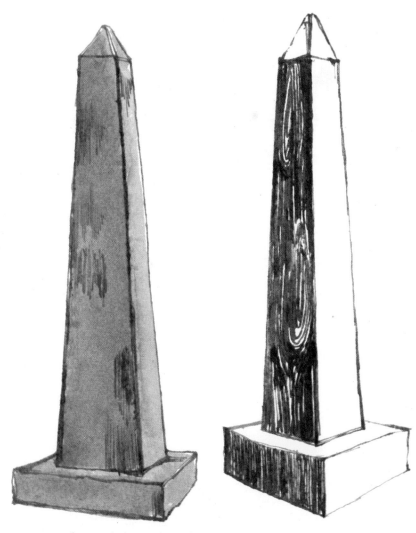

Decorate the sides of the obelisk.
Paint little pictures round it.
You could carve writing in the clay
with a little stick.

Index